by Di Pert
illustrated by Chantal Stewart

SCHOOL PUBLISHERS

Printed in the United States of America

ISBN 10: 0-15-350613-X
ISBN 13: 978-0-15-350613-0

Ordering Options
ISBN 10: 0-15-350598-2 (Grade 1 On-Level Collection)
ISBN 13: 978-0-15-350598-0 (Grade 1 On-Level Collection)
ISBN 10: 0-15-357759-2 (package of 5)
ISBN 13: 978-0-15-357759-8 (package of 5)

1 2 3 4 5 6 7 8 9 10   179   15 14 13 12 11 10 09 08 07 06

Cliff has long feet.
At school, he runs fast and
jumps a long way.

Cliff wants to do a new
thing.

At home, Liz says,
"Use your arms to swing."

4

"I can't hit the ball,"
says Cliff.

"Use your head,"
says Liz.

"I miss the ball every
time," says Cliff.
"Use your feet to swim,"
says Liz.

"I can swim fast!"
says Cliff.